The Fifties

All My Tomorrows	2
All The Way	4
Autumn Leaves (Les Feuilles Mortes)	6
C'est Si Bon (It's So Good)	8
Cherry Pink And Apple Blossom White	10
Cry Me A River	12
Dream Lover	14
The Great Pretender	16
The Green Door	18
High Hopes	20
It Doesn't Matter Anymore	22
It Only Hurts For A Little While	24
It's Nice To Go Trav'ling	26
I've Grown Accustomed To Her Face	28
Love Is A Many Splendoured Thing	30
Magic Moments	32
Mister Sandman	34
Only You (And You Alone)	36
Sing A Rainbow	38
A Teenager In Love	40
Thank Heaven For Little Girls	42
Volare	44
Whatever Will Be Will Be (Que Sera Sera)	46

Music arranged and processed by Barnes Music Engraving Ltd
East Sussex TN22 4HA, UK

Cover design by xheight Limited

Published 1995

All My Tomorrows

Words by Sammy Cahn / Music by James Van Heusen

Suggested Registration: Soft Rock
Rhythm: Vibraphone
Tempo: ♩ = 78

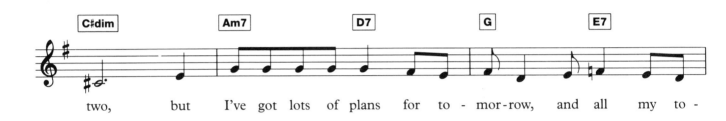

To - day I may not have a thing at all, ex - cept for just a dream or

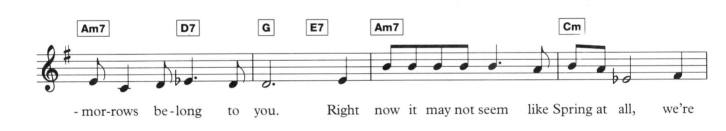

two, but I've got lots of plans for to - mor - row, and all my to -

- mor - rows be - long to you. Right now it may not seem like Spring at all, we're

drift - ing and the laughs are few, but I've got rain - bows planned for to -

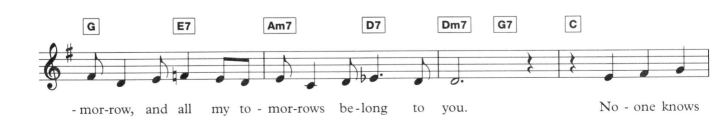

- mor - row, and all my to - mor - rows be - long to you. No - one knows

The International Music Network Ltd, Buckhurst Hill, Essex IG9 5NS

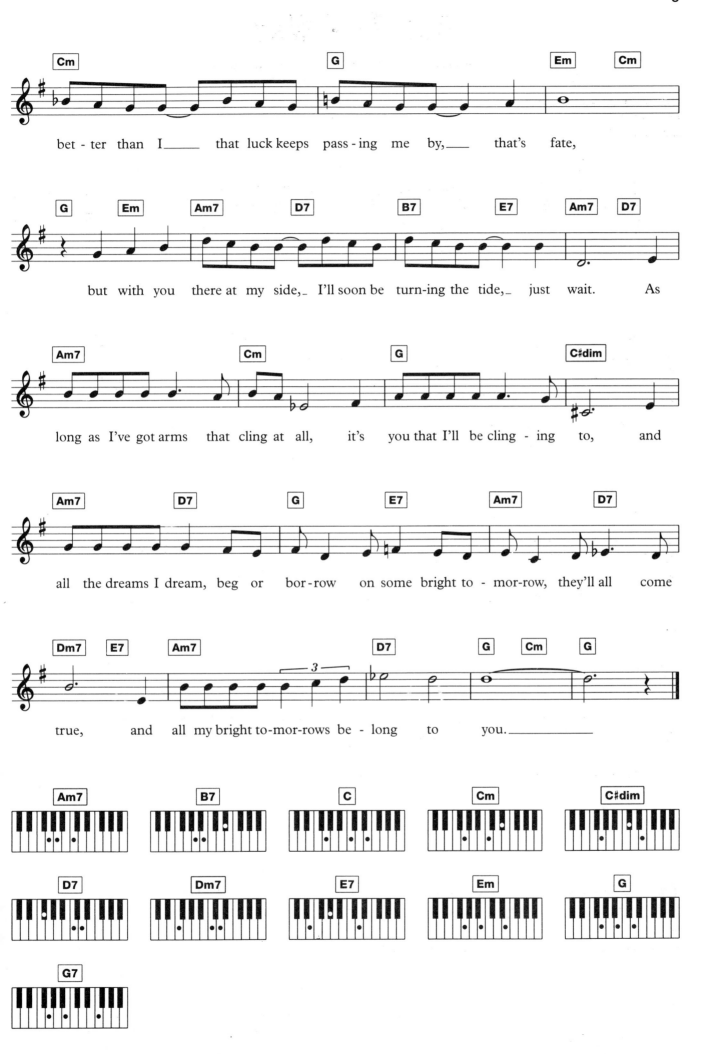

All The Way

Words and Music by Sammy Cahn and James Van Heusen

Suggested Registration: Piano
Rhythm: Slow Swing
Tempo: ♩ = 78

When some-bo - dy loves you, it's no good un - less he loves you all the

way. Hap - py to be near you, when you need some - one to cheer you

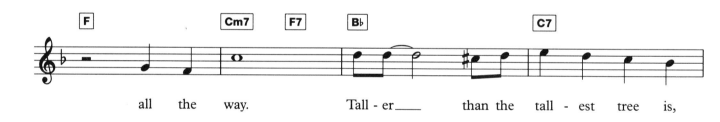

all the way. Tall - er___ than the tall - est tree is,

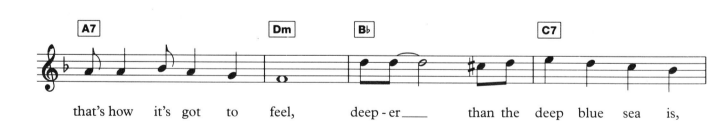

that's how it's got to feel, deep - er___ than the deep blue sea is,

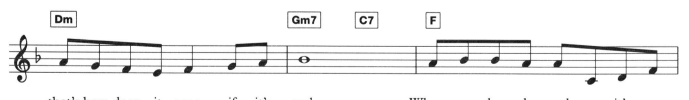

that's how deep it goes, if it's real. When some - bo - dy needs you, it's no

The International Music Network Ltd, Buckhurst Hill, Essex IG9 5NS

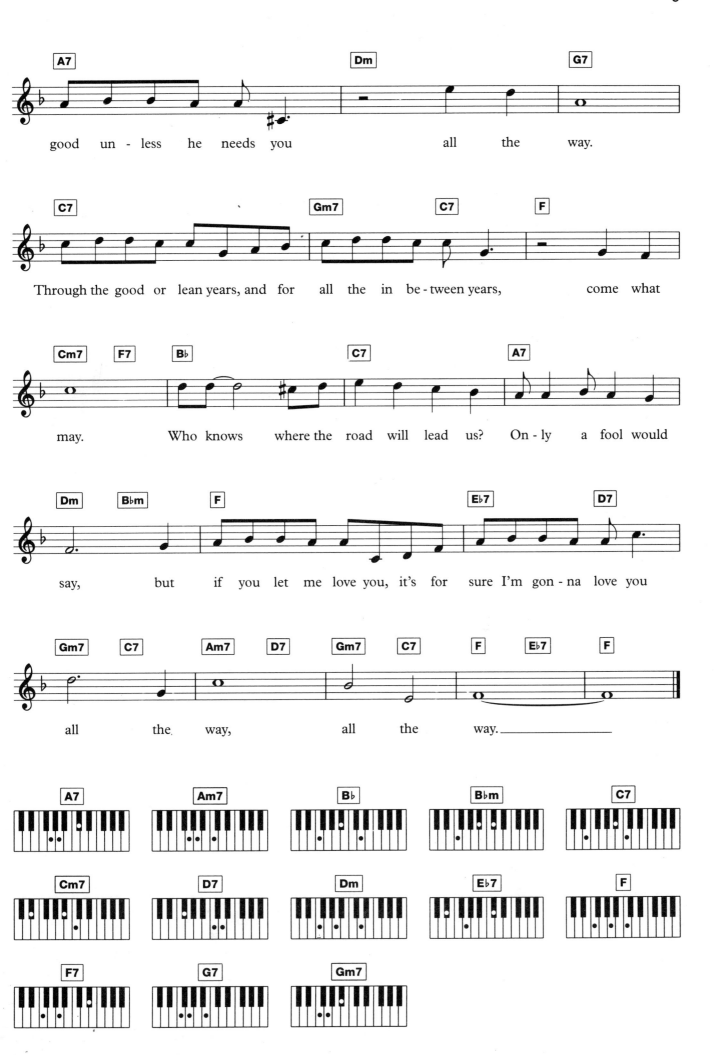

Autumn Leaves (Les Feuilles Mortes)

English Words by Johnny Mercer / French Words by Jacques Prevert / Music by Joseph Kosma

Suggested Registration: Clarinet
Rhythm: Slow Swing
Tempo: ♩ = 108

The fall - ing

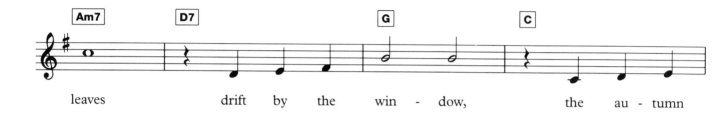

leaves   drift   by   the   win - dow,   the   au - tumn

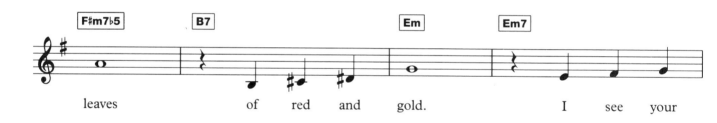

leaves   of   red   and   gold.   I   see   your

lips,   the   sum - mer   kiss - es,   the   sun - burned

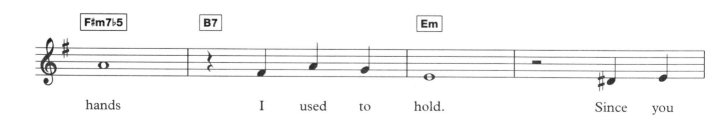

hands   I   used   to   hold.   Since   you

French lyrics and music © 1947 & 1995 Enoch et Cie

English lyrics © 1950 Ardmore Music Corp, France

Peter Maurice Music Co Ltd, London WC2H 0EA

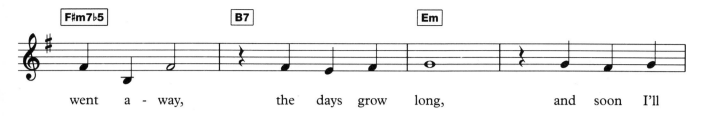

went a - way, the days grow long, and soon I'll

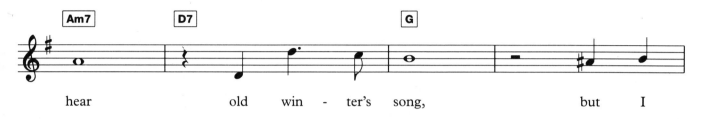

hear old win - ter's song, but I

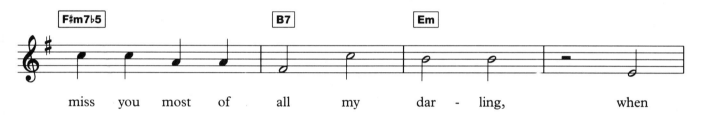

miss you most of all my dar - ling, when

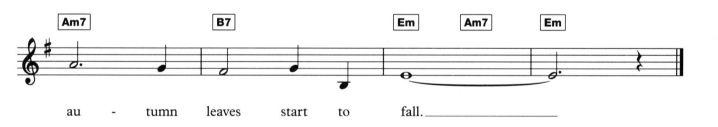

au - tumn leaves start to fall._____

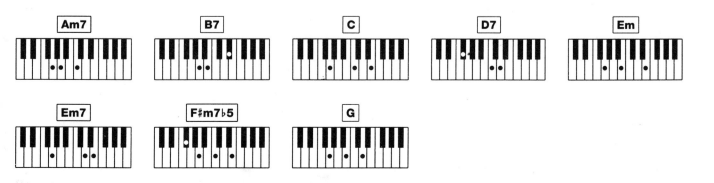

C'est Si Bon (It's So Good)

English Words by Jerry Seelen, French Words by Andre Hornez / Music by Henri Betti

Suggested Registration: Accordian
Rhythm: Swing
Tempo: ♩ = 132

'C'est si bon,' lov-ers say that in France

when they thrill to ro-mance, it means that it's so good.____

— 'C'est si bon,' so I say it to you like the french peo-ple

do, be-cause it's oh so good.____ Ev-ery

word, ev-'ry sigh, ev-'ry kiss dear,____ leads to

on-ly one thought, and it's this dear. It's so good,

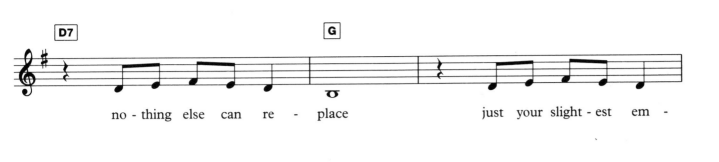

no - thing else can re - place   just your slight - est em -

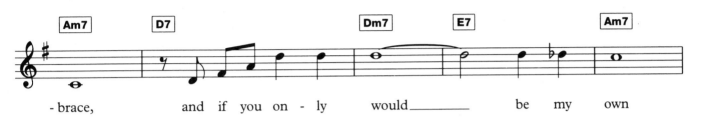

- brace,   and if you on - ly would_____ be my own

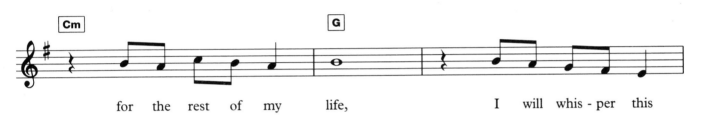

for the rest of my life,   I will whis - per this

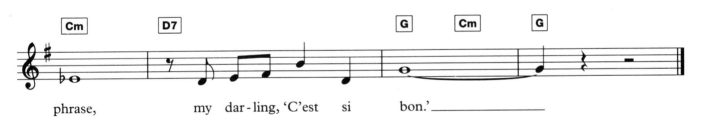

phrase,   my dar - ling, 'C'est si bon.'_____

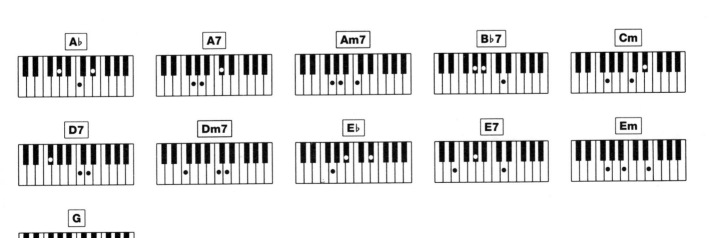

CHERRY PINK AND APPLE BLOSSOM WHITE

French Words by Jacques Larue, English Words by Mack David / Music by Louiguy

Suggested Registration: Acoustic Guitar
Rhythm: Rhumba / Latin
Tempo: ♩ = 132

It's cher-ry pink and ap-ple blos-som white   when your true lov-er comes your

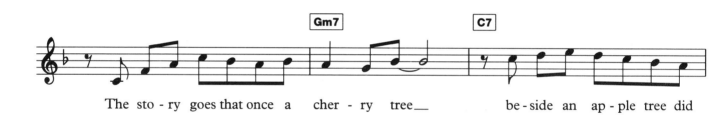

way,   it's cher-ry pink and ap-ple blos-som white   the po-ets say.

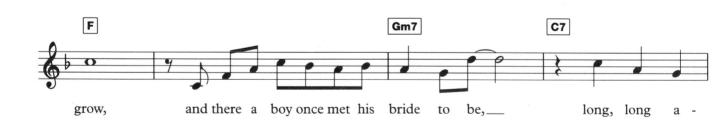

The sto-ry goes that once a cher-ry tree___   be-side an ap-ple tree did

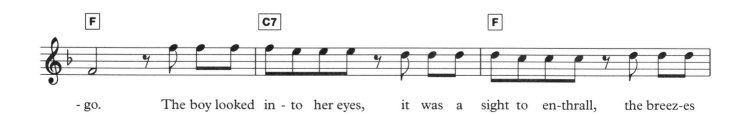

grow,   and there a boy once met his bride to be,___   long, long a-

- go.   The boy looked in-to her eyes,   it was a sight to en-thrall,   the breez-es

Warner Chappell Music Ltd, London W1Y 3FA

CRY ME A RIVER

Words and Music by Arthur Hamilton

Suggested Registration: Jazz Guitar
Rhythm: Slow Swing
Tempo: ♩ = 72

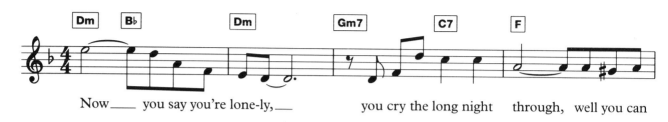

Now___ you say you're lone-ly,___ you cry the long night through, well you can

cry___ me a ri-ver, cry me a ri-ver, I cried a ri-ver o-ver you.

Now___ you say you're sor-ry___ for be-in' so un-true,___ well you can

cry___ me a ri-ver, cry me a ri-ver, I cried a ri-ver o-ver

you. You drove me,___ near-ly drove me out of my head,___ while

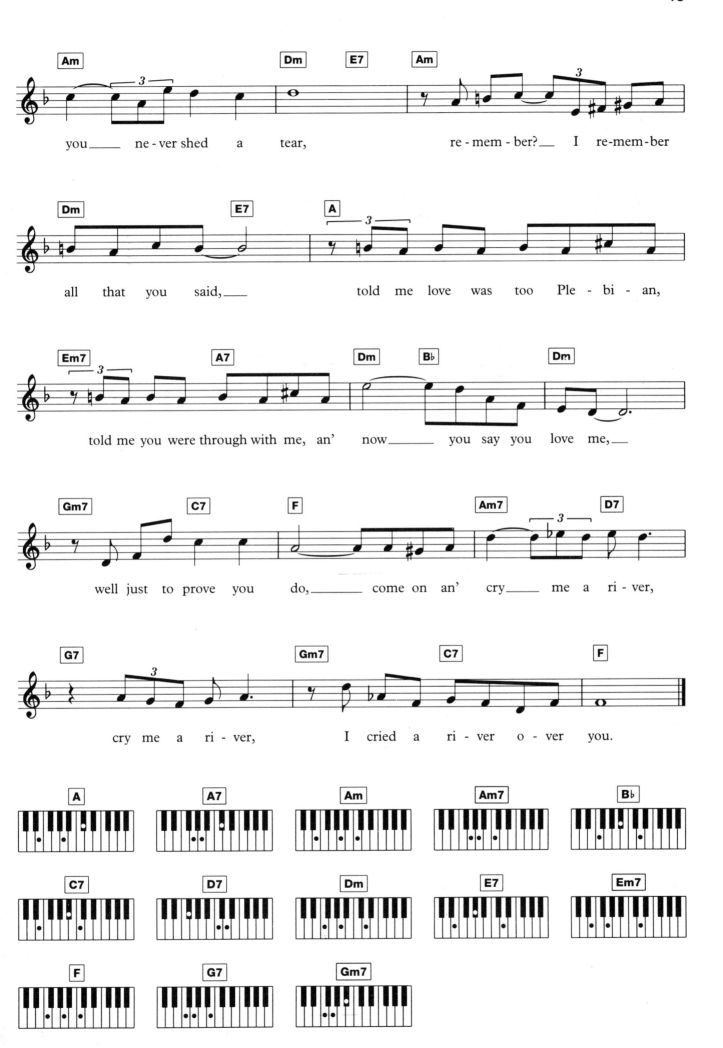

DREAM LOVER

Words and Music by Bobby Darin

Suggested Registration: Saxophone
Rhythm: 8 Beat
Tempo: ♩ = 132

Ev - ery night I hope and pray_____ a dream lov - er will

come my way,_ a girl to hold in my arms,_____ and know the ma - gic

of her charms, be-cause I want a girl to call__ my

own,__ I want a dream lov - er, so I don't have to dream a - lone.____

— Some day, I don't know how,_____ I hope you'll

The Great Pretender

Words and Music by Buck Ram

Suggested Registration: Saxophone
Rhythm: Slow Rock (6/8)
Tempo: ♩ = 70

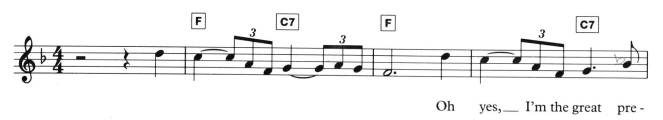

Oh   yes, ___ I'm the great pre -

- tend - er,   pre - tend-ing   I'm ___ do-in' well,   my   need   is   such ___ I pre -

- tend   too ___ much,   I'm   lone - ly,   but   no - one   can   tell.   Oh

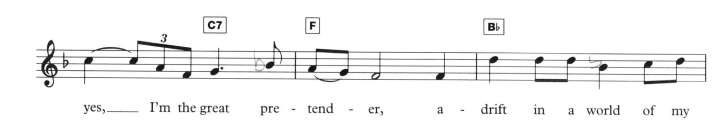

yes, ___ I'm the great   pre - tend - er,   a - drift   in   a   world   of   my

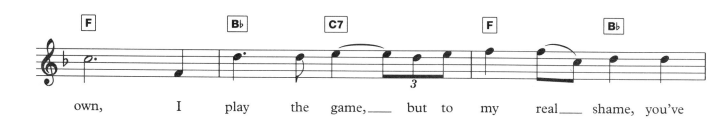

own,   I   play   the   game, ___ but   to   my   real ___ shame,   you've

The Green Door

Words by Marvin Moore / Music by Bob Davie

Suggested Registration: Saxophone
Rhythm: Pop Swing
Tempo: ♩ = 132

Mid - night, one more night with-out sleep - in', ___

watch - in' ___ till the morn - ing comes creep - in, ___

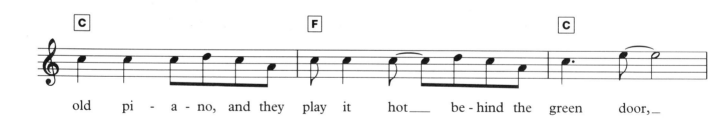

green door, _ what's that sec - ret you're keep - in'? ___ There's an

old pi - a - no, and they play it hot ___ be - hind the green door, _

don't know what they're do - in', but they laugh a lot ___ be - hind the

green door.__ Wish they'd let me in so I could

find out what's be-hind the green door.__ Mid - night,_

one more night with-out sleep - in',__ watch - in'__ till the morn-ing comes

creep - in,__ green door, what's that sec-ret you're keep - in'?__

Green door, what's that sec-ret you're keep - in'?__ Green door!

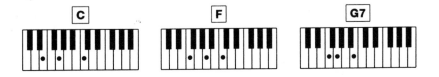

HIGH HOPES

Words by Sammy Cahn / Music by James Van Heusen

Suggested Registration: Clarinet
Rhythm: Swing
Tempo: ♩ = 128

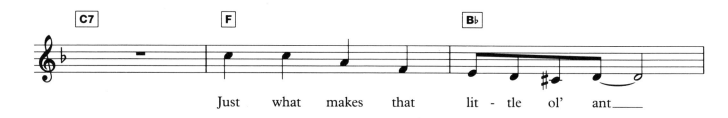

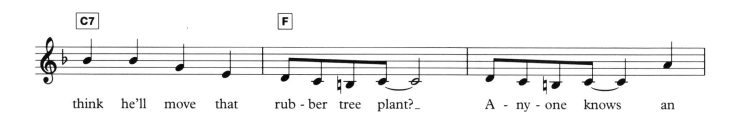

Just what makes that lit - tle ol' ant____

think he'll move that rub - ber tree plant?_ A - ny - one knows an

ant can't___ move a rub - ber tree plant, but he's got

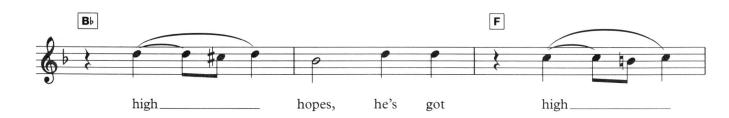

high_____ hopes, he's got high_____

The International Music Network Ltd, Buckhurst Hill, Essex IG9 5NS

hopes, he's got high ap - ple pie in the

sky_____ hopes, so a - ny time you're get - tin' low,

'stead of let - tin' go, just re - mem - ber that ant.

Oops! There goes an - oth - er rub - ber tree plant.

Oops! There goes an - oth - er rub - ber tree plant._____

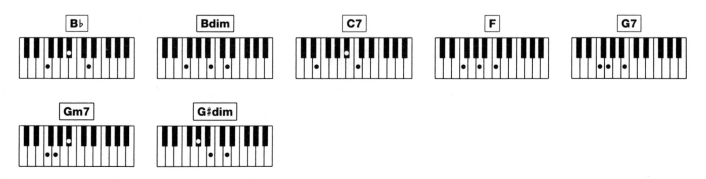

It Doesn't Matter Anymore

Words and Music by Paul Anka

Suggested Registration: Saxophone
Rhythm: Pop Swing
Tempo: ♩ = 196 125

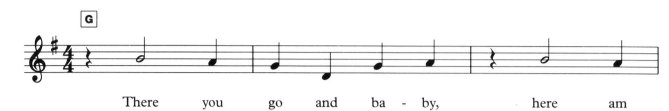

There you go and ba - by, here am

I, well, you left me here so I could sit and

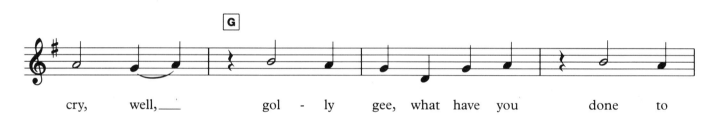

cry, well, ___ gol - ly gee, what have you done to

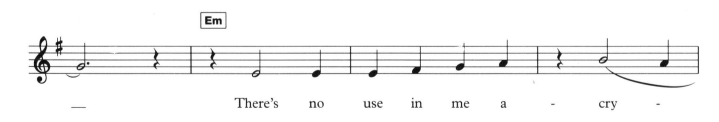

me? I guess it does - n't mat - ter a - ny - more. ___

___ There's no use in me a - cry -

- in', I've done ev - ery - thing, and now I'm

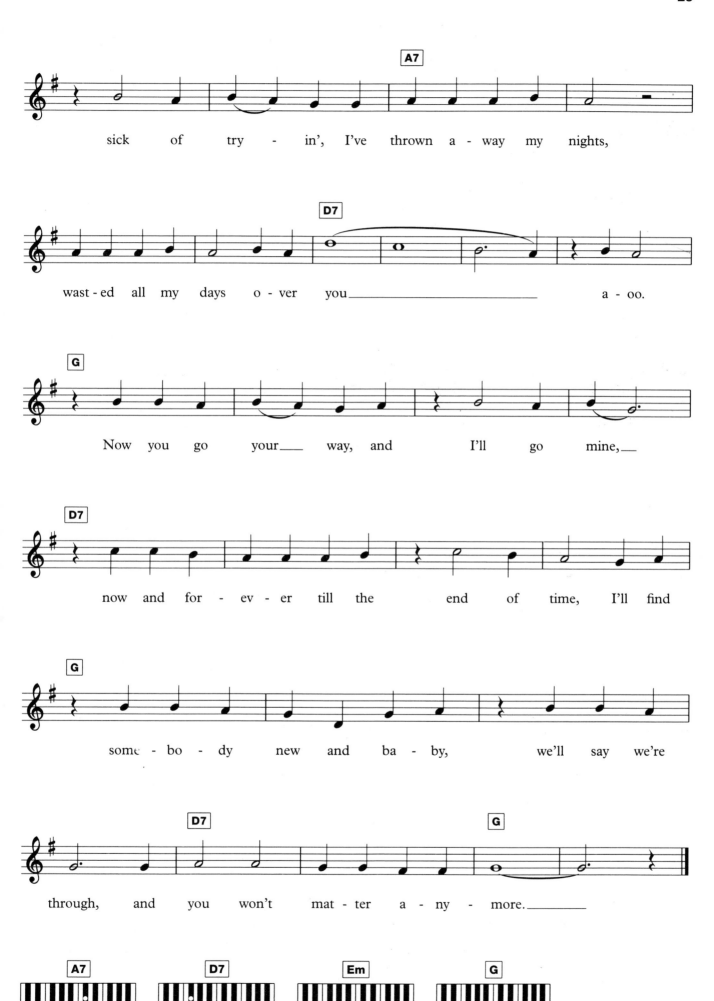

It Only Hurts For A Little While

Words by Mack David / Music by Fred Spielman

Suggested Registration: Strings
Rhythm: Waltz
Tempo: ♩ = 120

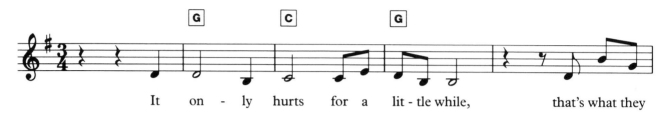

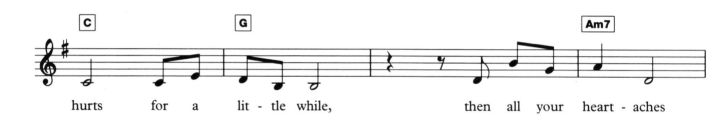

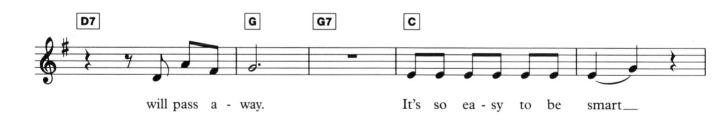

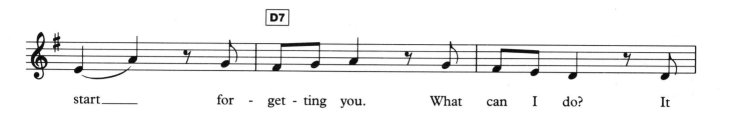

start_____ for - get - ting you. What can I do? It

on - ly hurts for a lit - tle while, that's what they

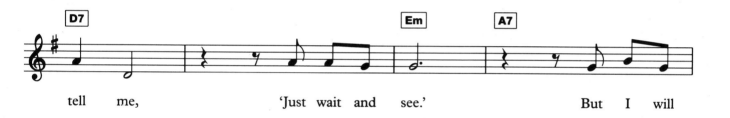

tell me, 'Just wait and see.' But I will

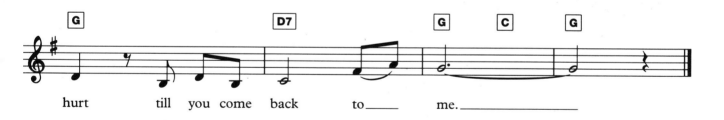

hurt till you come back to_____ me._____

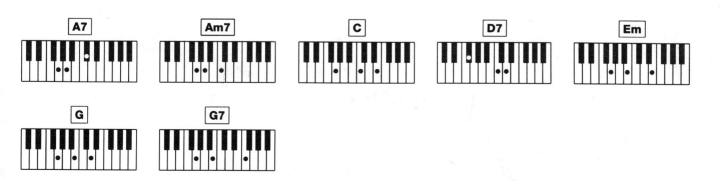

It's Nice To Go Trav'ling

Words by Sammy Cahn / Music by James Van Heusen

Suggested Registration: Accordian
Rhythm: Swing
Tempo: ♩ = 120

It's ve - ry nice___ to go trav - 'ling to Pa - ris, Lon - don and

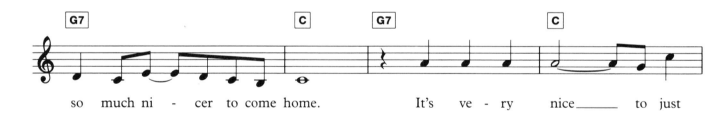

Rome, it's oh so nice___ to go trav - 'lin', but it's so much ni - cer, yes, it's

so much ni - cer to come home. It's ve - ry nice___ to just

wan - der the ca - mel route to I - raq, it's oh so nice___ to just

wan - der, but it's so much ni - cer, yes, it's oh so nice_ to wan-der back.

I'VE GROWN ACCUSTOMED TO HER FACE

Words by Alan Jay Lerner / Music by Frederick Loewe

Suggested Registration: Strings
Rhythm: Soft Rock
Tempo: ♩ = 78

I've grown ac - cus-tomed to her face,_____ she al - most

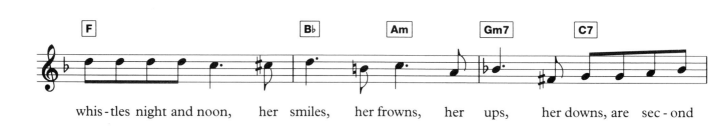

makes the day be - gin,_____ I've grown ac - cus-tomed to the tune she

whis - tles night and noon, her smiles, her frowns, her ups, her downs, are sec - ond

na - ture to me now,_____ like breath-ing out and breath-ing in._____

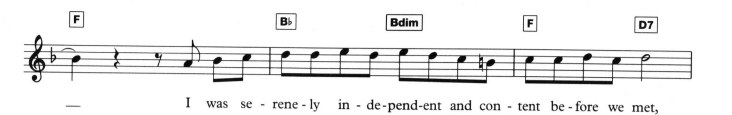

I was se-rene-ly in-de-pend-ent and con-tent be-fore we met,

sure-ly I could al-ways be that way a-gain? And yet, I've grown ac-cus-tomed to her looks, ac-

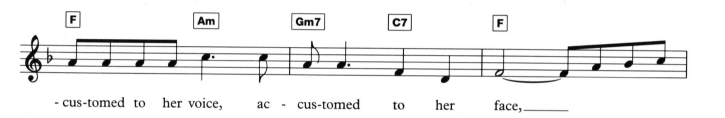

-cus-tomed to her voice, ac-cus-tomed to her face,____

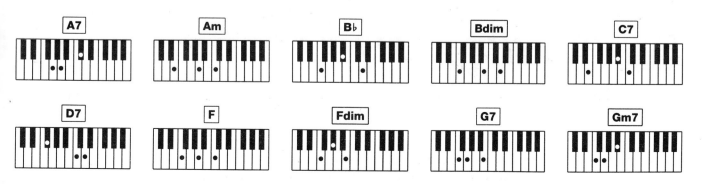

Love Is A Many Splendoured Thing

Words by Paul Francis Webster / Music by Sammy Fain

Suggested Registration: Strings
Rhythm: Soft Rock
Tempo: ♩ = 104

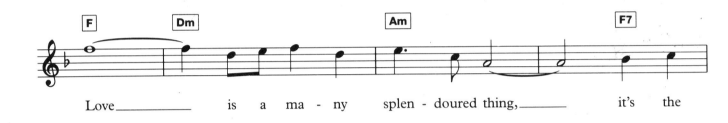

Love_____ is a ma - ny splen - doured thing,_____ it's the

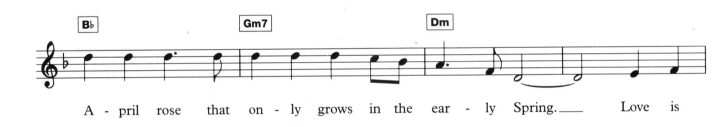

A - pril rose that on - ly grows in the ear - ly Spring.____ Love is

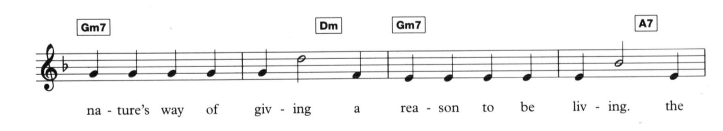

na - ture's way of giv - ing a rea - son to be liv - ing. the

gol - den crown that makes a man a king._____ Once_____

__ on a high and win - dy hill,_____ in the morn - ing mist two

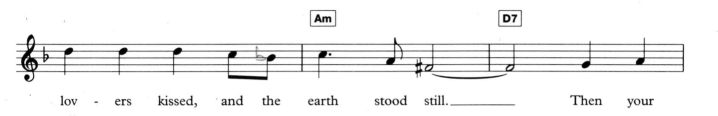

lov - ers kissed, and the earth stood still._____ Then your

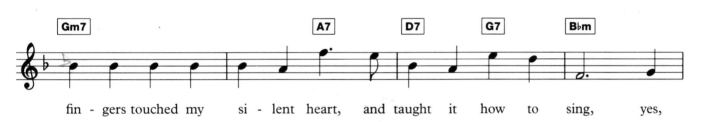

fin - gers touched my si - lent heart, and taught it how to sing, yes,

true love's_____ a ma - ny splen - doured thing._____

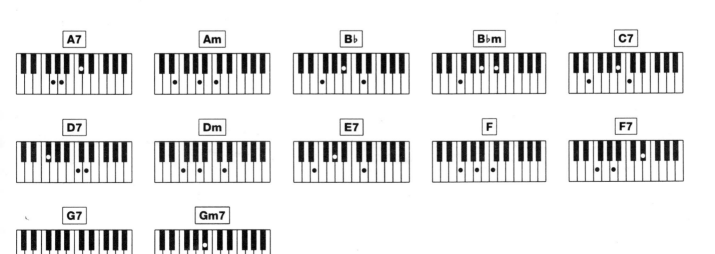

Magic Moments

Words by Hal David / Music by Burt Bacharach

Suggested Registration: Electric Piano
Rhythm: Shuffle
Tempo: ♩ = 94

Ma - gic mo - ments, mem-'ries we've been shar - ing, ma - gic

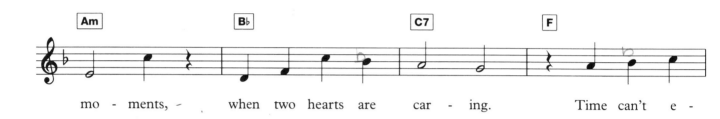

mo - ments, - when two hearts are car - ing. Time can't e -

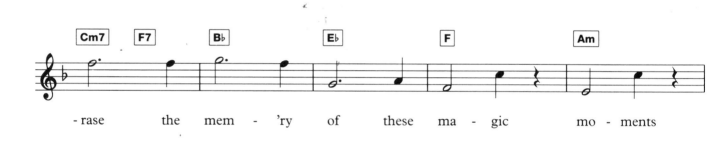

- rase the mem - 'ry of these ma - gic mo - ments

filled with love. I'll ne - ver for - get the mo - ment we

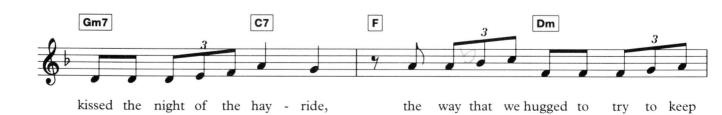

kissed the night of the hay - ride, the way that we hugged to try to keep

warm while tak - ing a sleigh - ride. Ma - gic mo - ments,

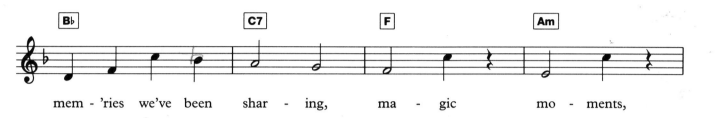

mem - 'ries we've been shar - ing, ma - gic mo - ments,

when two hearts are car - ing. Time can't e - rase the mem - 'ry

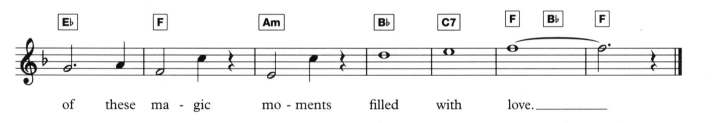

of these ma - gic mo - ments filled with love.

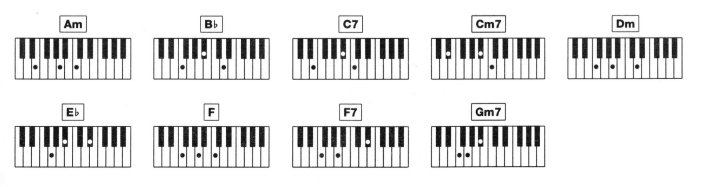

MISTER SANDMAN

Words and Music by Pat Ballard

Suggested Registration: Vibraphone
Rhythm: Swing
Tempo: ♩ = 200

Mis - ter   Sand - man,

bring me a dream,___   make her com -

-plex - ion   like peach - es and cream,___   give her two

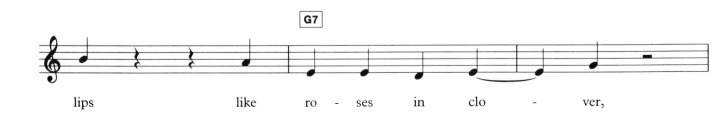

lips   like ro - ses in clo - ver,

Only You (And You Alone)

Words and Music by Buck Ram and Ande Rand

Suggested Registration: Trombone
Rhythm: Shuffle
Tempo: ♩ = 86

On - ly you _____ can make this world seem right, _____

_____ on - ly you _____ can make the dark - ness bright, _____

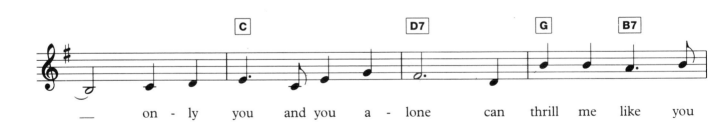

_____ on - ly you and you a - lone can thrill me like you

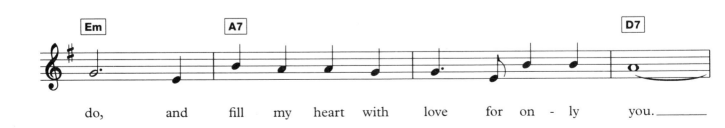

do, and fill my heart with love for on - ly you. _____

SING A RAINBOW

Words and Music by Arthur Hamilton

Suggested Registration: Celesta
Rhythm: Soft Rock
Tempo: ♩ = 87

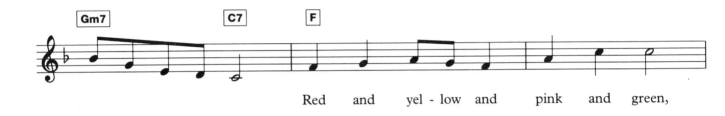

Red and yel - low and pink and green,

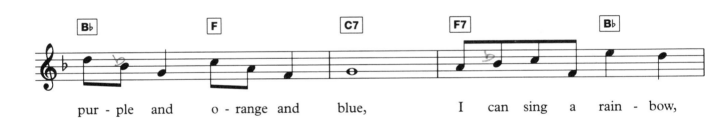

pur - ple and o - range and blue, I can sing a rain - bow,

sing a rain - bow, sing a rain - bow too.

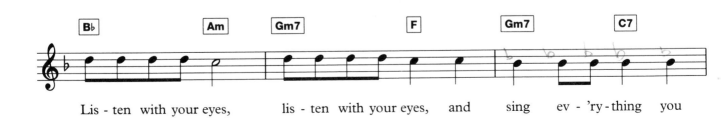

Lis - ten with your eyes, lis - ten with your eyes, and sing ev - 'ry-thing you

A Teenager In Love

Words and Music by Doc Pomus and Mort Shuman

Suggested Registration: Piano
Rhythm: 8 Beat
Tempo: ♩ = 168

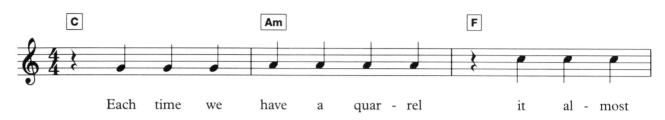

Each time we have a quar-rel it al-most

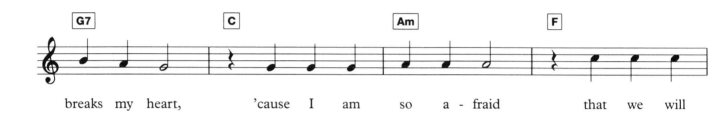

breaks my heart, 'cause I am so a-fraid that we will

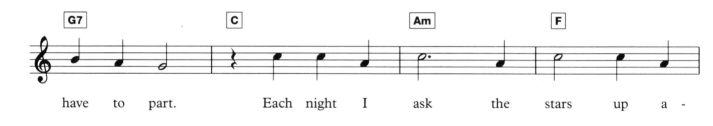

have to part. Each night I ask the stars up a-

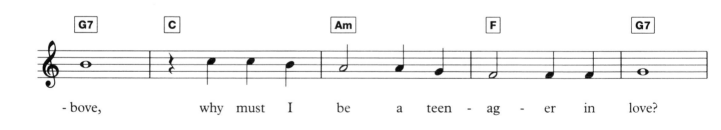

-bove, why must I be a teen-ag-er in love?

I cried a tear for no-bo-dy but you, I'll be a

lone - ly one if you should say we're through.

If you want to make me cry, that won't be so hard to do,

and if you should say good - bye, I'll still go on lov - ing you.

Each night I ask the stars up a - bove, why must I

be a teen - ag - er in love, in love?_____

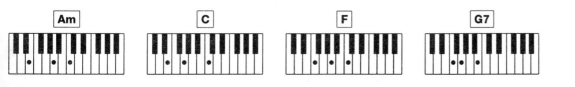

Thank Heaven For Little Girls

Words by Alan Jay Lerner / Music by Frederick Loewe

Suggested Registration: Accordian
Rhythm: Swing
Tempo: ♩ = 148

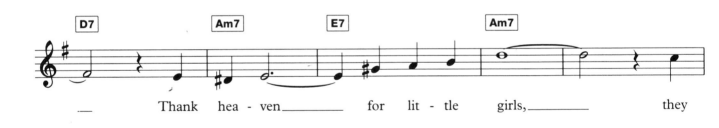

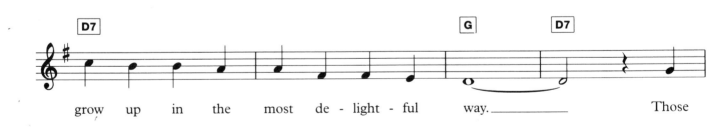

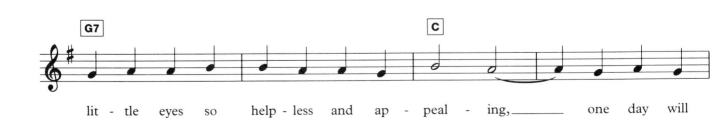

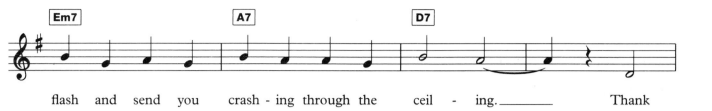

flash and send you crash - ing through the ceil - ing._____ Thank

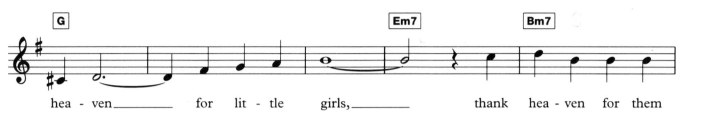

hea - ven_____ for lit - tle girls,_____ thank hea - ven for them

all, no mat - ter where, no mat - ter who, with -

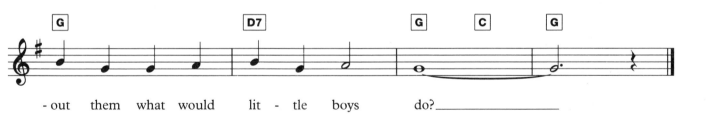

- out them what would lit - tle boys do?_____

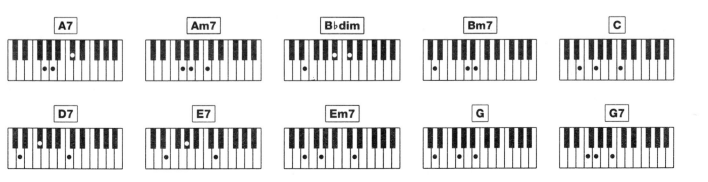

VOLARE

English Words by Mitchel Parish / Music by Donenico Modugno

Suggested Registration: Accordian
Rhythm: Swing
Tempo: ♩ = 144

Vo - la - re, _____ oh oh, _____ can - ta - re _____

_ oh oh oh oh. _____ Let's fly way up to the clouds, a -

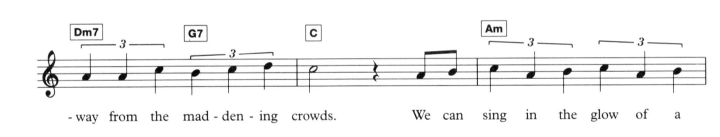

-way from the mad - den - ing crowds. We can sing in the glow of a

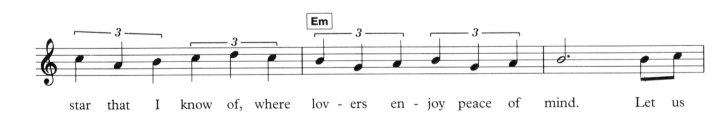

star that I know of, where lov - ers en - joy peace of mind. Let us

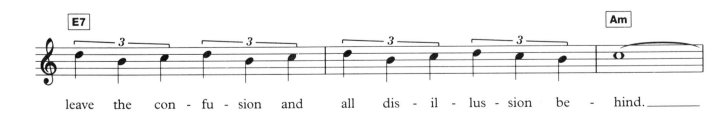

leave the con - fu - sion and all dis - il - lus - sion be - hind. _____

WHATEVER WILL BE WILL BE
(QUE SERA SERA)

Words and Music by Jay Livingston and Ray Evans

Suggested Registration: Clarinet
Rhythm: Waltz
Tempo: ♩ = 190

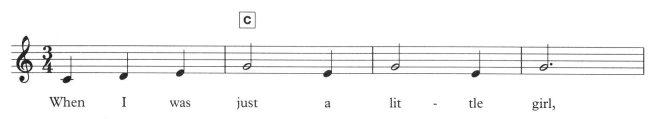

When I was just a lit - tle girl,

I asked my mo - ther, 'What will I

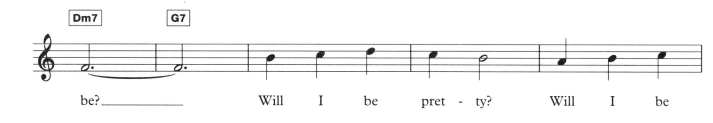

be?_____ Will I be pret - ty? Will I be

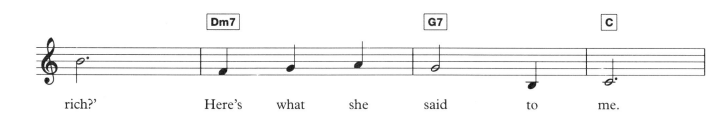

rich?' Here's what she said to me.

'Que se - ra, se - ra,_____ what -

THE EASY KEYBOARD LIBRARY

Also available in the Decades Series

THE TWENTIES
including:

Ain't Misbehavin'	My Blue Heaven
Ain't She Sweet?	Side By Side
Baby Face	Spread A Little Happiness
The Man I Love	When You're Smiling

THE THIRTIES
including:

All Of Me	The Lady Is A Tramp
A Fine Romance	Smoke Gets In Your Eyes
I Wanna Be Loved By You	Summertime
I've Got You Under My Skin	Walkin' My Baby Back Home

THE FORTIES
including:

Almost Like Being In Love	Sentimental Journey
Don't Get Around Much Any More	Swinging On A Star
How High The Moon	Tenderly
Let There Be Love	You Make Me Feel So Young

THE FIFTIES
including:

All The Way	Magic Moments
Cry Me A River	Mister Sandman
Dream Lover	A Teenager In Love
High Hopes	Whatever Will Be Will Be

THE SIXTIES
including:

Cabaret	My Kind Of Girl
Happy Birthday Sweet Sixteen	Needles And Pins
I'm A Believer	There's A Kind Of Hush
The Loco-motion	Walk On By

THE SEVENTIES
including:

Chanson D'Amour	Save Your Kisses For Me
Hi Ho Silver Lining	Take Good Care Of My Baby
I'm Not In Love	We've Only Just Begun
Isn't She Lovely	You Light Up My Life

THE EIGHTIES
including:

Anything For You	I Want To Break Free
China In Your Hand	Karma Chameleon
Everytime You Go Away	Nikita
Golden Brown	Take My Breath Away

THE NINETIES
including:

Crocodile Shoes	Promise Me
I Swear	Sacrifice
A Million Love Songs	Think Twice
The One And Only	Would I Lie To You?

THE EASY KEYBOARD LIBRARY